AF527006

Stories from Islam

Nuh and His Ark

Ziya Us Salam

Om SPARKS
An Imprint of Om Books International

It was late in the evening, and Rasheeda was tired. She put aside her walking stick, lay down on her charpoy, and drew a blanket over herself. A cool breeze was blowing. The sky was clear and the stars were shining. She felt relaxed.

Just as her eyes began to droop, her grandson, Salman came running to her. “Grandma, tell me another story!”

"No, not today, Salman, I am tired. I will tell you a story tomorrow," said Rasheeda, knowing full well that Salman wouldn't rest till his wish had been fulfilled.

"Please, Grandma, you are the best Grandma in the world! I won't disturb you tomorrow," Salman looked at his grandmother with earnestness.

How could Rasheeda say no to him? She sighed. “Promise me that you will be a good boy. You will obey God and….”

“Promise, Grandmother, I promise.” Salman was impatient, eager for another tale.

Rasheeda closed her eyes, took a deep breath and began, “After God created Adam, more children were born. Some grew up to be responsible men and women. They obeyed the command of Allah. Others, however, did as they pleased. They only cared about themselves. Allah was concerned about them. He did not want His people to suffer in Hell and decided to send someone to guide them.”

"I know! He was Prophet Mohammed," Salman said confidently.

"Not so fast, young man, not so fast. Prophet Mohammed was the last prophet of Allah. Before him, there were nearly 124,000 prophets and messengers."

“So many!” Salman exclaimed.

Rasheeda nodded, “Yes, so many. When a lot of people did bad deeds, Allah sent a prophet to them.

"One of these prophets was Nuh. Allah gave Nuh a long life–950 years! Prophet Nuh asked his people to obey Allah, to speak the truth; to not cheat others. Only a few people listened to Prophet Nuh, however. Most continued to be disobedient and sinful.

"One day, Allah asked Nuh to build an ark–a big boat. Nuh collected the best wood possible, joined the logs of wood together and built an ark.

"The ark took years to build. People laughed at him, but Nuh was determined. He continued his work faithfully and patiently. Finally the ark was complete. It was a large ark, with a lot of space for Nuh to store food and water. Allah asked Nuh to collect all the people who were obedient to Him in the ark, along with one pair of each animal."

"Then…" Salman gazed at his grandmother with his wide eyes. "Then?" Rasheeda smiled."Then there was thunder, lightning, and never-ending rain! The waters rose dangerously. The ark, however, sailed away. Bad people were not allowed inside the ark. Only good people were saved by Allah. He punished the naughty ones; all of them were swallowed by the water."

"I will be a good boy, Grandma! I will not cheat and will always obey Allah," Salman said, his mind full of boats and animals.